The Scale Of Things

The Scale of
FAMOUS JOURNEYS

Joanna Brundle

Crabtree Publishing Company

www.crabtreebooks.com

CRABTREE
PUBLISHING COMPANY
WWW.CRABTREEBOOKS.COM

Author: Joanna Brundle

Editorial director: Kathy Middleton

Editors: Emilie Dufresne, Janine Deschenes

Design: Jasmine Pointer

Proofreader: Crystal Sikkens

Prepress technician: Tammy McGarr

Print coordinator: Katherine Berti

All facts, statistics, web addresses and URLs in this book were verified as valid and accurate at time of writing.
No responsibility for any changes to external websites or references can be accepted by either the author or publisher.

Image Credits

All images courtesy of Shutterstock.com. With thanks to Getty Images, Thinkstock Photo and iStockphoto.

Front Cover – Emilia Ennessy, Colorlife, Ekaterina Kiriy, VectorSMD, Tancha, Mr. Luck, Krylovochka. 2–3 – natashanast. 4–5 – MicroOne, Sunnydream, Tanakax3, darsi. 6–7 – bilha golan, intararit, ONYXprj, Shtonado, avh_vectors. 8–9 – A7880S. 10–11 – AnnstasAg, Macrovector, Vector Icon Flat, Guaxinim. 12–13 – Sira Anamwong, N.MacTavish. 14–15 – robuart. 16–17 – natashanast, Janos Levente, Dzianis_Rakhuba, Pompaem Gogh, Bobrik74. 18–19 – Derplan13, robuart. 20–21 – Ziablik, eveleen, Bur_malin. 22–23 – Amanita Silvicora, Lorelyn Medina, Sunnydream.

Library and Archives Canada Cataloguing in Publication

Title: The scale of famous journeys / Joanna Brundle.
Other titles: Scale of travel
Names: Brundle, Joanna, author.
Description: Series statement: The scale of things |
    Previously published under title: The scale of travel. King's Lynn, Norfolk :
    BookLife Publishing, 2019. | Includes index.
Identifiers: Canadiana (print) 20190191872 | Canadiana (ebook) 20190191880 |
    ISBN 9780778776567 (hardcover) |
    ISBN 9780778776741 (softcover) |
    ISBN 9781427125286 (HTML)
Subjects: LCSH: Voyages and travels—Juvenile literature. | LCSH: Distances—Measurement—Juvenile literature. | LCSH: Size perception—Juvenile literature. | LCSH: Size judgment—Juvenile literature.
Classification: LCC G175 .B78 2020 | DDC j910—dc23

Library of Congress Cataloging-in-Publication Data

Names: Brundle, Joanna, author.
Title: The scale of famous journeys / Joanna Brundle.
Description: New York : Crabtree Publishing Company, 2020. |
    Series: The scale of things | Includes index.
Identifiers: LCCN 2019043482 (print) | LCCN 2019043483 (ebook) |
    ISBN 9780778776567 (hardcover) |
    ISBN 9780778776741 (paperback) |
    ISBN 9781427125286 (ebook)
Subjects: LCSH: Voyages and travel--Juvenile literature. | Distances--Juvenile literature.
Classification: LCC G175 .B78 2020 (print) | LCC G175 (ebook) | DDC 910.4--dc23
LC record available at https://lccn.loc.gov/2019043482
LC ebook record available at https://lccn.loc.gov/2019043483

Crabtree Publishing Company

www.crabtreebooks.com   1–800–387–7650
Published by Crabtree Publishing Company in 2020

©2019 BookLife Publishing Ltd.

Printed in the U.S.A./012020/CG20191115

Published in Canada
Crabtree Publishing
616 Welland Ave.
St. Catharines, Ontario
L2M 5V6

Published in the United States
Crabtree Publishing
PMB 59051
350 Fifth Avenue, 59th Floor
New York, New York 10118

CONTENTS

Words that are in **bold** can be found in the glossary on page 24.

INTRODUCTION

The scale of things means how one thing compares in size to another. In this book, we will compare famous journeys by their lengths, or how long they are. Get ready for a journey around the world— and even into space!

We will measure the lengths of the journeys in feet or miles and meters (m) or kilometers (km). A large school bus is about 45 feet (13.7 m) long. The Grand Canyon is about 277 miles (446 km) long. Use these measurements to help you imagine how long the journeys are.

The journeys in this book include famous competitions, new ways to travel, and exciting **expeditions**. Some measurements in this book are **approximate**. You can read the measurements that match the ones you learn in school.

In this book, you will see these symbols. **Each one stands for a different journey.**

Wright Brothers' flights

Marathon

Amundsen's expedition

Tour de France

Route 66

Atlantic Ocean

Trans-Siberian Railway

Amy Johnson's flight

Apollo 11

THE WRIGHT BROTHERS' FLIGHTS AND THE MARATHON

To design their plane, Wilbur and Orville copied the shape of birds' wings. They named the plane the Flyer.

Wilbur and Orville Wright were American **inventors**. They invented the first airplane. On December 17, 1903, they made the first-ever flights in a plane with an engine. On the fourth flight, Wilbur flew 852 feet (260 m).

852 feet (260 m)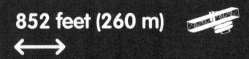

A marathon is a long-distance race. Participants run, walk, or use a wheelchair to travel just over 26 miles (42 km), or 137,280 feet (41,843 m). That's more than **160 TIMES** farther than Wilbur Wright's famous flight.

26 miles (42 km), or 137,280 feet (41,843 m)

THE MARATHON AND THE RACE TO THE SOUTH POLE

Many cities, including New York, London, and Beijing, hold a marathon each year.

People believe that the first-ever marathon was run in ancient Greece. A **messenger** ran from the city of Marathon to the city of Athens with news that a battle had been won.

26 miles (42 km)

↔

1,615 miles (2,600 km)

In 1911, Roald Amundsen led the first expedition that reached the South Pole, in Antarctica. His journey from the Bay of Whales to the South Pole and back again covered around 1,615 miles (2,600 km). That is the distance of almost 62 marathons.

South Pole

1,615 miles (2,600 km) round trip

Antarctica

Bay of Whales

THE RACE TO THE
SOUTH POLE
AND THE
TOUR DE FRANCE

Amundsen explored both the North and South Poles. His expedition to the South Pole in 1911 turned into a race against an English explorer called Robert Scott. Amundsen reached the South Pole 33 days before Scott.

2,175 miles (3,500 km) 🚲

←

The Tour de France is a famous bicycle race around France. The exact distance of the race changes each year, but it is usually around 2,175 miles (3,500 km).

The Tour de France is around the same distance as Amundsen's expedition and over 21 marathons joined together.

France

THE TOUR DE FRANCE AND ROUTE 66

The number of people who watch the race around the world is the highest for any yearly sporting event.

The first Tour de France was held in 1903. The race usually happens over 23 days in July. It has 21 different stages. The leader of the race at the end of each stage wears a yellow shirt for the next stage.

Route 66 was a famous highway in the United States. Called "the Main Street of America," it crossed eight states. When it was built, its length was around 2,448 miles (3,940 km) long. That's about as far as a Tour de France and ten marathons joined together.

2,448 miles (3,940 km)

ROUTE 66
AND CROSSING THE
ATLANTIC OCEAN

New York

Chicago

Santa Monica

ROUTE
66

The original
Route 66 ran from
Chicago, Illinois, to
Santa Monica, California.
It is no longer used as a
highway. Instead, it is a
historic road. Tourists visit it
to learn about U.S. history.

The distance by ship across the Atlantic Ocean from New York City to Southampton, in England, is over 3,579 miles (5,760 km). That is almost **ONE AND A HALF TIMES** as long as Route 66, or the distance of 138 marathons.

3,579 miles (5,760 km)

3,610 miles (5,809 km)

Southampton

Paris

In 1927, Charles Lindbergh was the first person to fly a plane *solo* across the Atlantic Ocean. His trip from New York to Paris, France, was around 3,610 miles (5,809 km) long.

Atlantic Ocean

2,448 miles
(3,940 km)

3,579 miles
(5,760 km)

CROSSING THE ATLANTIC OCEAN AND THE TRANS-SIBERIAN RAILWAY

Most people cross the Atlantic Ocean by plane or ship. But a man named Ben Lecomte is believed to have swam across the Atlantic Ocean in 1998. His journey covered 3,716 miles (5,980 km) and took 73 days.

Charles Lindbergh's flight across the Atlantic Ocean took 1 day and 9.5 hours. Ben Lecomte's Atlantic swim took about 52 TIMES longer.

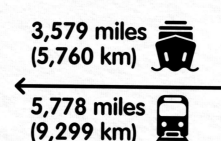

3,579 miles (5,760 km)

5,778 miles (9,299 km)

The longest railway in the world is the Trans-Siberian Railway. Its main line runs across Russia, between Moscow and Vladivostok. The journey covers around 5,778 miles (9,299 km).

Russia

5,778 miles (9,299 km)

Vladivostok

Moscow

The Trans-Siberian Railway is almost as long as one Atlantic Ocean crossing and one Route 66 joined together.

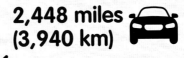

2,448 miles (3,940 km)

THE TRANS-SIBERIAN RAILWAY AND AMY JOHNSON'S FLIGHT

It takes over six days to complete the train journey from Moscow to Vladivostok. The train travels through mountains and forests. It also passes Lake Baikal. It is the largest **freshwater** lake, by the amount of water, in the world.

Amy Johnson's flight was almost as far as two journeys on the Trans-Siberian Railway.

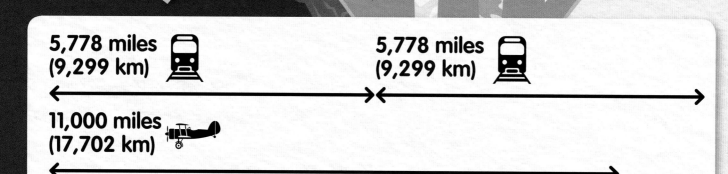

5,778 miles (9,299 km)

5,778 miles (9,299 km)

11,000 miles (17,702 km)

Amy Johnson was a pilot. In 1930, she became the first woman to fly solo from London, England, to Darwin, Australia. Her journey covered 11,000 miles (17,702 km).

England

└ **London**

11,000 miles (17,702 km)

Australia

└ **Darwin**

AMY JOHNSON'S FLIGHT
AND
APOLLO 11's FLIGHT
TO THE MOON

Amy Johnson had no GPS or radio link to talk with anyone on the ground, as pilots do today. She followed only basic maps to make her journey!

Amy Johnson took off from England on May 5, 1930, and landed in Australia 19 days later. Her plane, named Jason, was second-hand! She went on to set more records and was called "the Queen of the Air."

11,000 miles
(17,702 km)

↔

238,607 miles
(384,000 km)

←

On July 20, 1969, Apollo 11 became the first space flight to land **astronauts** on the Moon. The length of their journey from Earth to the Moon was around 238,855 miles (384,400 km).

The Apollo 11 flight to the Moon was more than **21 TIMES** longer than Amy Johnson's flight from London to Darwin.

APOLLO 11's FLIGHT
TO THE MOON AND
MARS LANDING

The astronauts took rocks and dust from the Moon back to Earth. Scientists studied them to learn more about the Moon.

Astronauts Neil Armstrong and Buzz Aldrin were the first humans to walk on the Moon. Millions of people around the world watched their steps on television.

The distance between Earth and Mars changes as each planet **orbits** the Sun. The shortest distance between the planets is around 33.9 million miles (54.6 million km). That is more than **141 TIMES** longer than the distance from Earth to the Moon.

Mars

Several uncrewed spacecraft **have** landed on Mars, but no humans have made the journey yet.

Earth

GLOSSARY

approximate Close to an exact measurement

astronaut A person who has been trained for space travel

expedition A journey with a certain purpose, such as to explore a new place

freshwater Water that does not have salt

GPS Short for Global Positioning System, a system that uses satellites to help people find their exact location

inventor A person who creates something new

measure Find out the size or amount of something

measurement The number we get after measuring something

messenger Someone who delivers news or instructions from one place to another

orbit To move in a curved path around a star or planet

scientist A person who studies and has a lot of knowledge about a type of science

solo Done by one person on their own

symbol A picture or mark that represents, or stands for, something

uncrewed spacecraft Space vehicles that do not have any humans on board. They are controlled by people on Earth.

INDEX